MW00654860

Poetry of My Love's Creation
Akashic – Afflicted – Awakened

B. Scott Dean
Editor: Annamarya Scaccia
Cover Art Concept: Maura E. Morris

Introduction

When it came time to write the introduction, I remember reaching out to my editor, stating, "Ugh! I don't know if I can do this. I hate talking and writing about myself."

Though, some who've met me would laughingly disagree and, to which, she sarcastically retorted, "Your entire collection is about you!"

What most no one knows is I began meditating and writing poetry at a young age. As I began to reflect on those years, I realized writing poetry wasn't an escape from the playground bullying I encountered as a young gay youth of the times.

On the contrary, it was an internalized, self-education of who I was, as well as an increased awareness of the world around me and my place within it. Unfortunately, those poems never saw the light of day, as I destroyed them right before high school graduation, thinking they were a "phase of my life."

Fast forward a few decades to 2020, when the pandemic forced the entire world into lockdown. I began to slowly disconnect, meditate, and write poetry again. Setting boundaries, providing myself the love I had neglected, and discovering my true authentic self became part of my daily rituals.

Then, the universe began to show itself to me in ways I hadn't seen since I was a child. As an adult, I was finally able to take a step back, slow my thought process enough to understand how the dots connected, and visualize everything in a different light, transmuting it all into the words of the poems you are about to read.

The inspiration for my writing ranged from a word, a lyric, or even a particular sound in a song I heard during my meditation bath that morning, to the rain pelting my skin as I ran the trail that afternoon, and to the spices enveloping my sense of taste and smell from the dinner I cooked that night. They would all combine in multiple ways to create images, colors, and emotions that could be expressed in two, three, or even four poems.

From a medical procedure conducted over the holiday season, which translated into one entire piece, to using my empathy to create and step into a specific type of relationship; of which, I've never experienced in my life, but was able to convey throughout the entire theme of poems within a section. At times, it became a bit overwhelming, but I was able to pace myself and collectively organize my thoughts and emotions.

Then, I began to comprehend, on a deeper level, that any and everyone who's ever interacted with me, no matter how miniscule or grandiose the experience, only knew me based on their perception of me at that time in my life.

These poems are an experience—my experience of love created, lived, and lost. I am, you are, and we are all experiences to be created and shared over the course of our lifetimes.

What you hold in your hands is forty years of experience from growing and learning about life, love, and myself.

This collection of poems is my heart and, with each turn of a page, a heartbeat. But, I hope, that with even one word read, your heart will skip a beat, and your love will continue to grow as mine did writing it.

Love Always,
Scottie

And once the storm is over, you won't remember how you made it through, how you managed to survive. You won't even be sure, whether the storm is really over. But one thing is certain. When you come out of the storm, you won't be the same person who walked in. That's what this storm's all about.

– Haruki Murakami, *Kafka on the Shore*

An akashic love...

Important encounters are planned by the souls long before the bodies see each other.

– Paulo Coelho

Elemental Devotion

He is my Water….
Deep enough to drown my sorrow.
Powerful enough to love like there's no tomorrow.

He is my Fire….
Determined enough to provide, for us, the best.
Charming enough to make me forget the rest.

He is my Earth….
Loyal enough that no one else can catch his eye.
Supportive enough to lift me past the clouds so high.

He is my Air….
Swift enough to push us forward into a future so bright.
Curious enough to want to know why and do what's
right.

He is….
…My Element.

The Dream

Last night,

I dreamt a dream like so many before.

I dreamt a dream where I kissed my lips to yours.

The Wish

Wished on a shooting star,
my soul took flight,
but got too close, like Icarus,
and I descended into night.

Crashed into you,
our souls became one,
creating a love for generations to come,
burning brighter than the sun.

The Flame

The sun may cease to rise.
The moon may never again
provide night's watch.

Life and its love affair with death may end,
never offering another gift again.

But,
know this certainty,
never doubt me and my love.

For,
you are my most
beloved godsend from above.

We are two in one, the same,
Twin Flame.

Signs of Love's Abandonment

My love, a youthful fountain,
ever flowing and ever growing,
hydrates the flesh and nourishes the soul.

My love, for granted taken:

A Scorpio's sting,
you'll wish you were dead.
A Cancer's pinch felt
from your Achilles to your head.

Slammed by a freight train
from raging Taurus, the bull.
Rammed by the horns of Aries,
piercing deep in the hull.

Water-bearing Aquarius'
electro-shock therapy of the soul.
Gemini's ***redrum*** twins
left you not knowing where to go.

Scales of Libra flipped,
the odds are never in your favor.
Sagittarius' charm retreated,
creates an addiction to savor.

Pisces will take you deep
and drown you in the abyss.
Capricorn leaves a calculated
feeling something's amiss.

Devoted Leo's broken pride
rips a heart from its chest.
Virgo's plan destroyed
makes you feel you lost the best.

Untitled (My Universe)

Your soul,
my world whole,
sends me deep into the cosmos.

Your smile,
new moon style,
keeps me alive through all life's phases.

Your love,
a shooting star above,
grants my nocturnal wishes.

Rêve céleste
(Celestial Dream)

La lune et les étoiles,
(The moon and stars,)

TU
(YOU)

et tes yeux radieux,
(and your radiant eyes,)

ES
(ARE)

le seul et unique
(the one and only)

MON
(MY)

désirs du ciel de minuit
(midnight sky desires)

POUR TOUJOURS.
(FOREVER.)

Nocturnal Secrets

Look at the moon in the sky above.

I tell it my secrets and of the one I love.

...realized in flesh

Life in itself has no meaning. Life is an opportunity to create meaning. Meaning has not to be discovered: it has to be created. You will find meaning only if you create it. It is not lying there somewhere behind the bushes, so you can go and you search a little bit and find it. It is not there like a rock that you will find. It is a poem to be composed, it is a song to be sung, it is a dance to be danced. Meaning is a dance, not a rock. Meaning is music. You will find it only if you create it. Remember it.

– Osho, *The Perfect Master, Vol. 2, Chapter 4*

You, My Home

My favorite trip ever made
was the way to your heart.

Knowing together forever
we'll be
is the very best part.

I knew I found
home
when our souls conversed.

You are my sun and moon
amongst the stars.

You are my universe!

You, Me, We

Scents of
You
Transport
Me
to where
We
meet.

A kiss from your lips
hydrates my yearning heart.

Embers igniting our passionate souls
provides love everlasting for the two of us.

New World Love

Release your love,
set yourself free,
unafraid, with me.

Antediluvian molds that created we,
shall crumble and remake anew
with our soul's love,
for all the new world to see.

Feu d'âme
(Soul Fire)

Que cherchez-vous?
(What are you searching for?)

Est-ce toi ou moi?
(Is it you or me?)
La lune ou une étoile?
(The moon or a star?)
Est-ce ici ou là?
(Is it here or there?)

Que la lumière du feu de l'âme
(May the light of soul fire)
conduis-toi à moi.
(lead you to me.)

Et nous
(And we)
allumerons le monde en feu
(will light the world on fire)
avec l'étreinte de l'amour.
(with love's embrace.)

Toujours l'amour
(Love Always.)

Wrapped in Your Love

Come, the bed is cold.

Lie on top of me,
my warmest blanket.
Intertwine with me,
extending our love to all four corners.

Roll me over.
Envelope me with you,
as we gaze towards the moon.

You're all around me…

Our hearts beat in sync
with love's internal rhythm.

A calm breath on my neck,
knowing you're still here.

Body heat protects me
from old man winter's bite.

Wrap me in you all night
and into the day.

There's no one else for me...

…not now…not ever…no way…

Trace of Luck

Drops of morning rain
pound the windowpane,
waking me in your arms.

A calming breath,
from your peaceful slumber,
syncopates my heartbeat
to a restful pace.

I begin to trace
the four-leaf clover
over your heart.

Wishing, as I did,
from the very start,
for a love with you
that will never part.

Feeling Your Memory

Let my fingers discover
every inch of you.

Sketching you in my mind
while meticulously
remembering all your
curves and edges

When the time comes
for us to part,
I simply must close my eyes
and feel you in my heart.

A Deeper Love

When you love me,
you must swim in the deep.

You need to know
how to let yourself go.

Give yourself to me.
Don't be afraid to drown.

Breathe me in.
Let me be your oxygen.

In the Deep

When your soul is too deep to explore…

…for those who swim along the shallow shore.

Growing Love

Our love is built
from jaded pasts,
hope,
and honesty.

As a seedling sprouts
deep within the ground,
so does our love grow in secrecy.

Yesterday & Today

Yesterday,

I gave you my love,
the stars and the moon.

Today,

you broke my heart
and made me a crazy loon.

Love Me Not

This invisible force pulling me towards you,
I've felt before in another lifetime or two.

Penetrates the air, suffocating my senses,
weakens my knees, and tunnels my vision.

Though, each time I traverse
the labyrinth to your heart,
the minotaur is there
to knock me out from the start.

You strum a ballad on my heartstrings
all night long, playing that old,
unrequited love song.

But, two can play this charade,
as you pluck the petals from my perennial bud,
which makes me think you already forgot.

When springtime comes 'round,
with magnificent glory,
I'll bloom again, and...

...you'll be left with the love-me-nots.

An afflicted love…

Affliction comes to us, not to make us sad but sober; not to make us sorry but wise.

– H.G. Wells

Drunk on You

We are each other's pleasure
and each other's pain,

but I needed to see you once again.

We both knew we wanted it all,
when you pinned me against the wall.

To feel you in my soul;
two made whole.

Eternally Forgotten Sunshine

Thinking of you, as you turn the key
to unlock the vault, but I put a halt to it all.

Finally, I grabbed the key
and turned it myself.
Opening the lid,
I exposed all that I hid
from the world and myself.

Memories and words,
a house of cards built,
from a love lost years ago.

Waiting for a strong wind
to carry them away,
or me to give them a simple blow.

I had to let you go, to set ourselves free.

Like eternally forgotten sunshine,
an empty space in my mind,

moving me forward…

…leaving you behind.

Give Me A Clue

Searching the letters for a clue,
cause I want to know,
what happened between me and you.

Never wanted us to go our own way,
but you don't seem to want to stay.

You already know where I stand,
so I need to know:

Where do you want us to go?

Rescue Me

Drenched my heart
with this bottle of wine.

Numbed every layer skin.
Devoid of all emotion within.

Getting dizzy up so high
lying to myself that you'll come around.

Would I feel anything?

Would you rescue me....

if

I

fell

to

the

ground?

Triggered

A shotgun cocked.
A trigger pulled.
A blast to my head.

WAIT!

Did you think I was dead?

Memories of us,
minuscule grains of sand,
displaced light years away.

Across the universe.
Amongst the stars.

Left me weak in stature.
Beginning again,
from the start.

Solace was found
within the strength of my heart.

Reflections

I began my day not knowing
how it would all unfold.

Truth be told!

Only time would tell,
after an emotional exchange
of words, tears shed, and
beratements of selfish yell,
when the truth would remove
me from this vacant shell.

For it was my own truth I sought,
with the ticket I bought,
to learn how I'd become both
a player and an observer.
Two in one, the same,
in this game of blame.

After a biased apology sent,
I realized how the story went.
Conversational smoke and haze
hid a mirror preventing you to see.
The verbal accusations spewed
were but a reflection of you, not me.

Wool Sweater

You tried pulling the wool over my eyes.

The wool from my very own sweater.

And from that moment forward, I knew,

I could do much better than you.

Borrowed Time

My heart and soul I gave to you,
when no one else ever knew.

Thought we'd go long
in this game of love and life,
but how was I supposed to know that
what our love did lack,
on that night you came back,
and forever,
left my immune system under attack.

Stared me dead in the face,
denying the cheat,
but your pride was too thick
to admit defeat.

L'affliction de l'amour
(Love's Affliction)

Après des années à me sentir bien,
(After years of feeling fine,)
ta présence s'est fait connaître
(your presence made known)
quand tu m'as poignardé par derrière.
(when you stabbed me from behind.)

Pénétrant plus profondément qu'avant,
(Penetrating deeper than before,)
mon dos me fait toujours mal de toi en train de voler
(my back still throbbing from you robbing)
quel était le mien.
(what was mine.)

Se promener, la carapace d'un homme,
(Walking around, the shell of a man,)
chercher le sens de la vie encore une fois.
(searching for life's meaning once again.)

Vers le bas j'ai tourné le verre et se mit à boire.
(Downward I turned the glass and began to drink.)
Pourquoi nous ne pouvons pas nous laisser aller.
(Wondering why we can't let each other go.)

Avec un amour comme le nôtre,
(With a love like ours,)
personne ne peut jamais savoir.
no one may ever know.)

A Dipsomaniac Love Affair

Ribs cracked by your words,
tortured was my drunken soul,
with no other place to go, had I, but

...down...
...down...
...down...

the rabbit hole.

Charming slander from your tongue,
without a simple thought.
Intoxicatingly bruised, was I,
from the alcohol you bought.

Taken for granted, my love, I could tell.

My only options given:
Is this my heaven, or is this my hell?

As the day drank into night,
the night sobered into day.

One perplexing question,
my inebriated mind continued to convey:

How can we make amends when we burn the candle at both ends?

555

When I got the call,
I didn't want to hear,
I didn't want to believe at all.

All of it so surreal,
as I rushed to the scene.
All I could let out
was a silent scream.

Hunched over the steering wheel,
with nary a breath of life.
The cop stood there
telling me you were alright.

But why did you have to die that night?

My heart was completely ripped out of my chest.
I thought, 'Well, there goes all my happiness.'

All these years, I know you've been with me....

...hearing you...feeling you...

My man,
this guardian angel who still loves me so.

In the physical world
I knew you had to go, so I could grow.

Growing

You,
my fated twist,
my catalyst,
from which to grow and learn,
throughout all the joy and all the burn.

What a reciprocity it was,
the witty banter,
the slanders of pain.
I'd go back in time
to relive it all again.

Instead,
with a pull of the reins
and a neigh of the horse,
I knew better for myself,
to take charge
and change the course.

In solitude,
with clearer vision
and a settled mind,
I let it all go,
leaving the past…

…behind.

Dark Night of the Soul

In the still, dark of night,
I did not hear the phone.

...ring, ring...
...ring, ring...

Awoke in a state of despair,
as the nightmares fleed my mind.

Reached across the bed and
there, my love, I did not find.

Flew across the room, peering out the window,
to the only place I knew, at this hour, he'd go.

Rays of moonlight highlighted faint tears
rolling from his eyes, as he stared back at mine.

I started to cower like a dying flower,
as my gaze began to lower, ever slower.

There, my love, did hang by a rigid noose
from the thick branch of our elderly spruce.

Snapped his neck by the rope, so hard and tight.
My spirit went numb and broken was my might.

Drowned

I drowned myself in
sorrow and misplaced tears.

I drowned myself in
uncertainty with many regrettable fears.

This misery,
unbeknownst to me,
I kept hidden all these years.

When, I wish,
I would've drowned myself in you.

A Loss for Words

Staring at the flame.
Meditating in the bath.

Music's soothing beat
numbing the drum in my ear.

Voices in my head
begin their celebratory dance,
as I drift deeper into a trance.

Random thoughts come and go.
Disappearing ink on my soul.

With nothing to write, except this:

My heart becomes void of inspiration.
My mind hopes for a revelation.

Then, amongst the celebration, a voice called out to me,

'These are your words, your voice, your melody.'

...loss and salvation enmeshed

Maybe you have to know the darkness before you can appreciate the light.

– Madeline L'Engle

The Most Painful...

The point at which I loved
you most was when I said,

"GOODBYE."

Live Out Loud

Living a life dying inside,
because you're too afraid
to talk about the feelings you hide.

Speak out, if you can,
receive a helping hand,
an attentive ear,
whether you're far or near.

Shades of You

My aura turned a violet hue
that night, many years back, when I met you.
Found my royal prince charming,
who couldn't find it in himself to harm me.

Each morning, as bright as the sun,
I woke with a golden shine so brand new.
Every night, a silver lining, brought out
the sensuous beast within.

With a spectrum of orange flare, tempers raged
throughout all the tumult and strife.
Smooth, red velvet within my veins,
flowed eternal love from me to you.

But, that day when all was lost,
my eyes turned a permanent shade of blue.

Désir
(Longing)

Chaque nuit pendant que je dors,
(Every night as I sleep,)
les rêves de toi et de notre amour dansent dans ma tête.
(dreams of you and our love dance through my head.)

Te sentir si loin,
(Feeling you so far away,)
alors que tu te tiens juste à côté de mon lit.
(though you're standing right next to my bed.)

...Des larmes qui roulent...
(...tears rolling...)
...Le cœur fait mal...
(...heart hurting...)

Les pensées commencent à inonder mon esprit,
(Thoughts begin to flood my mind,)
alors que je parle avec vous dans mon sommeil.
(as I talk with you in my sleep.)

Vous demandez pourquoi la mort est venue pour vous
(Wondering why death came for you)
et l'amour que nous avions si profond.
(and the love we had so deep.)

A Kiss From Love Lost

Our love shined brighter
than the sun until the day he died.

This left my soul bereft
until no more tears could I cry.

As I stand on the balcony,
a thunderstorm brings a downpour of rain

Pelting my lips, rolling down my cheek,
it permits me to feel him all over again.

A kiss from love lost:

A
numbing,
bittersweet
pain.

Only Time

We can

fall in love with,

fight against,

hope for,

dream about,

anything…

...except time.

(Only time will tell.)

A Place

I know a place,
past the eyes and beyond the soul.
Everything is fleeting,
no grip strong enough to hold.
Too dark for any light,
devoid of all effusiveness.

...so open...

...so empty...

...so cold...

A few times before, I swam in the shallow.
Once, I even swam in the deep.

As sand sinks through the hourglass,
I could feel the life,
from my body,
slowly seep.

Knowing it wasn't my time,
I fought tooth and nail
to retreat my heart
from my impending heaven...

...or impending hell.

Untitled (Wounds)

Wounds,
where insults
slashed my spine,
have no more room
for your slander.

Swift wings now grow.

To new heights, I soar, rising above it all.

An awakened love...

It is only in our darkest hours that we may discover the true strength of the brilliant light within ourselves that can never, ever be dimmed.

– Doe Zantamata

lIFe

If only...
I hadn't come out
as straight, bi, or gay.
...but, I did.

If only...
I hadn't finished college,
or never moved so far away.
...but, I did.

If only...
I hadn't met you leaving my life
compromised until the day I die.
...but, I did.

If only...
I hadn't put you, any of you, down,
knowing my fate would come around.
...but, I did.

If only...
I hadn't learned from my mistakes,
I might never have learned to forgive myself.
but, I did.

If only...
...but, I did.

Misinformation Society

All this knowledge
in the palm of our hands.

Yet, to so dumb, numb,
we've become.

Plug it in and connect'em,
but don't let'em get
into your cerebellum.

Video killed the radio star.
TV rots your brains.
The internet of things, but
d'you even know who you are?

Friend against friend.
Foe against foe.
Where is humanity going to go?

Let that *(E)*go.
Set your spirit free.

Rise above and transcend.
Be who you were meant to be.

The Beast Within

Have

you

ever

tried

to

destroy

what

hides

deep inside

in

order

to

survive?

Metamorphosing

Over the past 3-6-5,
what a tug-of-war it's been
being dead and alive.

It's always darkest before dawn.
Most calm before the storm.
You saw the light ignite in my eyes.

The oceans rise and
to the ways of old,
a demise.

So much devastation and debris,
left behind me.
Raw and exposed, I go,
into a future not even god knows.

This change occurring all around and inside.
No place to run. No place to hide.

My body shakes,
as earthquakes,
along the fault lines.

The soothing *Ohms*
transcend the spirit
and elevate the mind.

Rising

Lying amongst the ashes, deafening silence
and blinding darkness surround me.

Wondering,

as a flickering light permeates
this empty space,

I turn around to see…

ME!

A reflection of what once was,
scattered on the floor.
My soul's flame rekindled
anew in my flesh cocoon.

What a sight to behold,
as I begin to witness
my spirit's perpetual metamorphosis.

Miroir Kintsugi
(Kintsugi Mirror)

D'innombrables pièces brisées.
(Countless shattered pieces.)

Vérités et amours.
(Truths and loves.)

Mensonges et promesses non tenues.
(Lies and broken promises.)

Imperfections de quelqu'un qui était autrefois.
(Imperfections of someone who once was.)

Maintenant, rendu entier, reflétant une âme
(Now, made whole, reflecting a soul)
à ce que quelqu'un a créé de nouveau.
(to that someone created anew.)

What You See, What You Get

Walking towards me,
I could see in your eyes,
a life filled with
regret and despair,
much happiness and love,
but constant hope and repair.

As you stopped,
I continued
my inquisitive stare.

Then,
I turned to walk away from…

…the mirror.

Windows

Our flesh and bones
will weather and change
from life's toll.

Though,
our astute and effusive eyes
will forever remain
the windows to the soul.

Resilience

Obstacles laden throughout life's path,
a very important rationale do hath.

To break you down and watch you fall?

(NO!)

To educate, resonate, and rise above it all.

(SO!)

One day at a time, let's go the distance.

Learn and grow the provided way,
or be doomed to repeat another day.

Remembrance

There comes a point in our lives, a time,
when it all so quickly seems to fade.

An age.
A year.
A decade.

Each of you, a memory:

Cherished,
Loved,
& Learned.

Etched forever on my soul
and in my mind,
lingering like the essence
of fine wine.

Untitled (Balance Is Key)

Ask the universe
to love and understand,
not to judge and command.

Balance is key,
even when you take a stand.

Know Yourself, First

Throughout my life,
especially in the past year,
I learned to accept and love
"***Him***" and "***Her***" wholeheartedly.

So, you can't pick and choose
the parts of me,
if you want to love
and love me unconditionally.

He, the soft-shelled crab,
with a heart of 24-karat gold.
She, the prideful lioness,
who can't easily be sold.

Like the phoenix,
I will rise and fall
and rise again.

But, sorry ladies,
though pretty and sexy,
my desire still lies with men.

Live Your Life

To live life with your senses,
is to live in spiritual awareness.

To live life with your soul,
is to live in unconditional love.

But,
to live life with your entire being,
is to live in complete gratitude.

Transcendence

Close your eyes.

Look up.

Breathe.

See with your soul.
Don't let your mind take control.

Elevate and transcend.
Let the energy flow.

Manifest That Shit

Do not live in the past,
where regret and depression lie.

Do not live in the future,
where fear and anticipation are high.

Live in the present!

...breathe...
...focus...
...have faith...
...rest...

Let that shit manifest!

...live...
...love...
...learn...
...pray...

Be thankful every day!

You're never too young, or too old.
Be honest, loving, and bold,
for it will come back to you tenfold.

...illuminates and manifests

I am the master of my fate; I am the captain of my soul.

– William Ernest Henley, *Invictus*

MOTHER
(for my mom)

of us all,
wake us with the breath of life.

Our fertile and barren playground,
nourished and famished from your bosom.
Through tranquil and turbulent waters,
satiated thirsts and sorrows drowned.

Unconditional Love

Your womb, from birth to death,
our heaven and our hell.
With the Father we know, in time,
your love's balance revealed.

Disciplined Adoration

Unbeknownst to us,
when all comes due, you,
our place of eternal slumber
we shall return,
as it is all within your

NATURE

FATHER
(for my dad)

of us all,
build our lives with blocks of truth and rationale.

From day to week to month to year,
conceptual restrictions leave much to fear.
Anticipate the worst and hope for the best,
but give unto pendulum's swing the rest.

tick, tock...tick, tock

Yesterday is expired, out-of-stock
Tomorrow could be, live for
Today, as nothing is free.

Be present and unguard your love
to share with the world.
For with the Mother, we know
love's balance by not the extent of time.

tick, tock...tick, tock

Through is the only way out
and how it will work itself in the end,
with patience and

TIME

Whiskey In A Teacup
(for my sister)

Whether it's a sweet tea,
iced or hot, or a whiskey shot,
you better believe
she'll "***tell you what***".

This sister of mine,
my first best friend in life.

A daughter, an educator,
a loving mother, and a loyal wife.

Me, the slight antagonist
of her childhood,
because she always knew
when I was up to no good.

Every step of the way,
she'd call me out on my shit,
but I never hated or despised her.

Not then.
Not now.
Not one little bit.

In fact, as the scent of wisteria swiftly fades
with the memories of yesterday,
I love her more and more every day.

A Spade Is A Spade
(for my bother-in-law)

When it comes to our family,
you've got to have thick skin.
But, with his charm and quick wit,
he made his way in.

Married my sister,
heart and soul,
providing for his family
the life never had.

Protector of his brood,
the one they call dad.

This brother of mine,
equal parts refined wine and ice-cold beer.

But,
let me make myself clear!

There's a soft spot for the
special ones in the life he's made.

Though,
never one to sugarcoat,
He'll always call a spade a spade.

Be A Unicorn
(for my niece)

I know a young woman
who stepped outspokenly
into the world.

A far cry
from the trepidatious,
little, baby girl.

Making life her own,
with much creativity for her,
the world, to adorn.

Once, by her I was told,
if nothing else can you be…

…Be a unicorn!

Never let go,
never lose sight of who you are.
The world is your oyster,
my little pearl.

You are its shooting star!

King Of The Jungle
(for my nephew)

Stand out from the crowd
atop the highest cliff
and roar, mighty lion.

In this life,
you can make your mark,
when your bite
is as strong as your bark.

Do what's right!
Live your life
according to your own light.

Never settle for less!
Be the best throughout all
life's trials and tests.

Don't let it take control,
but go your own pace,
Dylan Trace.

JE SUIS
(I AM)

mortel et immortel
(mortal and immortal)
chair et esprit
(flesh and spirit)
masculin et féminin
(masculine and feminine)
clair et sombre
(light and dark)
indépendant et dépendant
(independent and dependent)
fort et faible
(strong and weak)
intelligent et ignorant
(intelligent and ignorant)
vrai et faux
(right and wrong)
confiant et timide
(confident and diffident)

JE SUIS HUMAIN
(I AM HUMAN)

Avec toutes mes imperfections acceptées,
(With all my imperfections accepted,)
mon équilibre découvert,
(my balance discovered,)
mon moi authentique révélé.
(my authentic self is revealed.)

L'AMOUR
(LOVE)

Though, I must confess, each one of us is a uniquely individual, lovingly beautiful, imperfectly perfect, lifelong mess…

…keep going…you are loved!

– B. Scott Dean

The End

Made in the USA
Monee, IL
24 July 2021

73774922R20095